Seek and Find
CITIES

Written by **Kate Baker** • Illustrated by **Sandra de la Prada**

... and my name is Bird.

Introduction

Meet our intrepid travellers, Cat and Bird. They've spent all year planning an amazing trip – a city-hopping tour around the world! They've packed their bags and are ready to go, but they need your help.

In each city, there are all kinds of things to spot. Look out for the icons on every page. They'll tell you what you need to find. It may be some tasty festival food, a traditional hat, a souvenir, or one of the local people or animals.

You'll need to hunt high and low, peep inside buildings and search in among the crowds. Leave no stone unturned! And don't forget to look for Cat and Bird in every city too.

All set? Then let the adventure begin . . .

The answers, plus even more things to spot, can be found at the back of the book.

Ice Rink

TORONTO, CANADA

It's winter in Toronto, the perfect time to try one of the favourite local pastimes – ice skating. Wrap up warm, put on your skates and give it a whirl!

The ice rink in Nathan Phillips Square is one of the busiest in the city.

Things to Spot

Orange earmuffs
A pair of ear warmers will come in handy in the cold and snowy winter weather.

Beaver
These buck-toothed, flat-tailed rodents are Canada's national symbol.

Moose
There's a moose on the loose! Not a real one though, a cuddly toy.

Ice hockey stick
Someone has lost their hockey stick. Can you help them find it?

 Dreamcatcher
These good-luck charms were first used by the indigenous Ojibwe people.

 Maple taffy
This wintertime treat is made from sweet maple sap and snow, then served on a stick.

 Snowshoes
These special shoes look a bit like tennis rackets and help you to walk on the snow.

 Inuksuk
Can you spy this Inuit statue? It's made from stones piled on top of one another.

New Year's Eve

NEW YORK CITY, USA

Welcome to New York – the city that never sleeps. The streets are humming with people celebrating under the dazzling lights of Times Square. As the clock strikes midnight, everyone cheers and claps. A new year has begun!

COMING SOON TO THEATERS

MILKSHAKE

ORIGINAL

The New Year fireworks display in Times Square is one of the most spectacular in the world.

TOUCHDOWN!

GER & FRIES

DONUTS

CENTRAL PARK

NEW YORK

Things to Spot

Clock and ball
Just before midnight, a giant ball is lowered from the clock to mark the start of a new year.

Big Apple
Did you know that New York City is also known as the Big Apple?

Policeman
This policeman is eating a doughnut – a popular New York City treat!

Cheerleader
Can you spy the cheerleader waving her pom-poms?

Pretzel
A pretzel is a type of bread made with dough and shaped into a twisted knot.

American footballer
American football is one of the country's favourite sports.

Souvenir t-shirt
Can you find the person wearing this souvenir t-shirt?

Foam hand
Search the crowds for this big foam hand with a pointy finger.

Day of the Dead

MEXICO CITY, MEXICO

This vibrant festival takes place each year on November 1st and 2nd – All Saints' Day and All Souls' Day. It is a time to remember family members who have died and to celebrate their lives.

Things to Spot

Smart skeleton
To help the dead feel at home, people paint their faces like skulls and dress in old-fashioned clothes.

Altar
Altars are decorated with flowers, candles and photos. Can you find this one?

Bread of the dead
Sweet bread shaped like a skull or a cross is a popular offering placed on the altars.

Pair of shoes
Other offerings include toys, clothes and shoes that once belonged to the dead family member.

Throughout Mexico, people hold parties and parades and leave offerings on specially built altars to welcome their lost loved ones back into the realm of the living.

Water jug
The dead will be thirsty after their long journey from the spirit world!

Pozole stew
This traditional stew is made from meat, onion, chilli peppers and limes.

Mariachi band
The band have lost each other in the crowd – can you help reunite them?

Aztec emperor
The festival was first celebrated hundreds of years ago by the Aztec people.

Actors dressed as Inca nobles, priests and townsfolk reenact the old Inca procession through the cobblestone streets.

Things to Spot

Sun god
The sun god Inti is usually represented as a sun with a human face.

Inca emperor
The actor playing the Inca emperor is carried on a golden chariot by pallbearers.

Inca priest
The Inca priests wear magnificent robes and pray to Inti for a good harvest.

Mandolin
People jump and dance as musicians play flutes, drums and mandolins.

Inti Raymi

CUSCO, PERU

Founded by the Inca people, who lived here hundreds of years ago, this festival is held in honour of the sun god, Inti. It takes place around the winter solstice and marks the time when the days begin to get sunnier and the coming of the harvest.

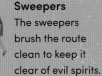 **Sweepers**
The sweepers brush the route clean to keep it clear of evil spirits.

 Bowl of chicha
People carry offerings of flowers, corn and chicha (a drink made from maize).

Puma statue
The puma was a sacred animal to the Inca. It was a symbol of great power and strength.

 Condor
The Inca believed that the condor bird carried the souls of the dead to heaven.

Carnival

RIO DE JANEIRO, BRAZIL

It's Carnival time in Rio – one of the most exciting festivals in the world. Crowds of people in colourful costumes are stomping through the streets, dancing and drumming to the samba beat. Come and join the parade!

Things to Spot

Carnival float
This float has been made to look like a toucan, one of Brazil's most beautiful birds.

Pink drum
A big drum called a surdo is used to keep a steady beat.

Samba whistle
The band leader toots on a samba whistle at the beginning and end of each song.

Red shaker stick
Special sticks with metal jingles are shaken in time with the music.

This lively carnival is held each year at the beginning of Lent. It's known for its samba music, which involves lots of drumming, jangling bells and whistles.

Monkey
In Rio, cheeky capuchin monkeys sometimes sneak into homes and steal fruit!

Footballer
Football is the most popular sport in Brazil. They have lots of famous players.

Yellow headdress
Rio is renowned for its carnival costumes with fancy feathers and sequins.

Lost flip-flop
Someone has lost their flip-flop in the crowd! Can you find it, and its owner, too?

Marketplace

MARRAKESH, MOROCCO

Our next stop is Djemaa el Fna – a bustling square in the medieval city of Marrakesh. There's lots to see and things to buy. There are acrobats, dancers, flute players and drummers. You can have your fortune told, your teeth pulled out, or sit and listen to storytellers spinning tales from years gone by!

There are all sorts of
treasures to be found,
from painted plates to
silver teapots, spices,
silks and slippers.

Things to Spot

Water sellers
Water sellers with
fringed hats jangle
cups together to
attract customers.

Set of false teeth
You can even visit a
dentist and choose
a brand-new set
of teeth!

Golden teapot
In Morocco, people
love to drink tea with
friends and family.
It is served in fancy
teapots like this one.

Boiled snails
These snails have
been boiled in a
broth with herbs and
spices. Delicious!

Green slippers
These traditional
slippers have been
hand made and are
called babouches.

Krakebs (castanets)
Can you find the
musician shaking a
pair of krakebs in
time to the music?

Star lantern
The markets are
filled with pretty
lanterns. This one
looks like a star.

Chameleon
This sneaky colour-
changing lizard
sometimes helps itself
to the market food.

The Pyramids of Giza

CAIRO, EGYPT

Rising out of the golden desert, the pyramids of Giza were built thousands of years ago for ancient Egyptian kings and queens. People come from all over the world to peep inside these magnificent tombs.

The tombs were once filled with objects for the pharaohs to use in the afterlife but over the years they have been raided by thieves. Today, you can buy gifts that look like the ancient treasures.

Things to Spot

Papyrus scroll
Papyrus is a kind of paper made from reeds used in ancient Egypt for writing.

Sand bottle
Bottles filled with desert sand are a popular souvenir. This one has pyramids inside.

Statue of Anubis
Anubis was the Egyptian god of the dead. He guarded the gates of the underworld.

Falcon
The falcon was a sacred bird to the Egyptians and thought to have protective powers.

Statue of Isis
Isis was a caring goddess who protected the sick and helped crops to grow.

Egyptian ibis
This long-necked bird is said to be the reincarnation of Thoth – the god of knowledge.

Egyptian mummy
An Egyptian mummy wrapped up in bandages is being a tourist for the day. Can you find it?

Archaeologist
Archaeologists are scientists who study objects from the past.

The Nairobi National Park on the edge of the city is home to all kinds of animals, including giraffes, lions and leopards.

Things to Spot

Lion sculpture
This wooden carving is shaped like a lion – the largest of Africa's big cats.

Zebra mask
Zebras look a bit like stripey horses. They are hunted by lions and crocodiles.

Maize cob
Look out for street vendors selling fresh fruit and grilled corn cobs.

Kikoi
This lady is using a traditional cloth called a kikoi to carry her baby on her back.

Maasai Market

NAIROBI, KENYA

Are you ready to haggle? This colourful market is crammed
with hand-crafted souvenirs made by the local people.
There are wooden carvings of wild beasts, paintings,
drums and tribal masks. What will you buy first?

Jewellery maker
Can you see the lady
threading beads to
make jewellery?

Baobab tree
This strange-looking
tree with a bulging
trunk grows on the
African grasslands.

Maasai warrior
The Maasai people live
on the African plains in
houses made from mud
and sticks.

Tribal mask
Wooden masks
were used by African
tribes to scare away
their enemies.

Trafalgar Square

LONDON, UK

Jump aboard a big red bus and see the sights of London Town. In the heart of the city is Trafalgar Square – popular with people-watchers, street performers and pigeons!

In the middle of the square is a statue called Nelson's Column. It stands 52 metres (170 feet) tall and is guarded by four giant lions made of bronze.

Things to Spot

Telephone box
England is known for its bright red phone boxes. The colour red was chosen to make them easy to spot.

Crown jewels
These precious jewels worn by British kings and queens are kept in the Tower of London.

Corgi
One of the Queen's corgis has escaped. Can you help return it to Her Majesty?

Street performer
This street performer is painted gold and looks like he's hovering in mid-air!

Palace guard
This souvenir looks just like one of the guards that stand outside Buckingham Palace.

Big Ben
Big Ben is the name of the huge bell that chimes inside London's famous clock tower.

Two lion statues
According to legend, the lions will come to life if Big Ben chimes thirteen times!

Red fox
London is home to thousands of foxes. One was once spotted riding on a bus!

You can see for miles from up here!

What will do you next? Are you brave enough to creep through the haunted house?

Things to Spot

Toffee apple
This traditional fairground food is sticky and sweet and tastes delicious!

French baguette
These long bread sticks are baked fresh each morning.

Artist's easel
Paris was once home to some of the world's greatest painters.

Arc de Triomphe
Keep your eyes peeled for a picture of this well-known Paris landmark!

Funfair

PARIS, FRANCE

It's summertime in beautiful Paris, and the fair is in town.
Take a spin on the merry-go-round then whizz down the
giant slide. Hold on to your beret and away you go!

Accordion
An accordion is an
instrument with keys like
a piano and bellows that
you squeeze.

Can-can dancer
Paris is famed for its
high-kicking dancers
with pretty frilly skirts.
Can you can-can?!

Black cat
Parisians love their
rat-catching cats. Can
you see this one eyeing
up the pigeons?

Hook-a-duck stall
This fairground game
involves hooking
rubber ducks using a
special fishing rod.

Christmas Market

MOSCOW, RUSSIA

Christmas is a magical time in Moscow. A blanket of snow covers the ground, and the city's famous Red Square is brimming with stalls selling festive treats – from wooden toys and woollen hats to hot tea and ginger biscuits!

Things to Spot

Snow Maiden
Look out for the Snow Maiden. If you've been good, she may have a gift for you.

Samovar
A samovar is a bit like a big kettle. It is used to boil water for making tea.

Space dog toy
In 1957, a Russian dog called Laika became the first animal to orbit the Earth!

Hand muff
A cosy hand muff will help to keep you warm in the snowy weather.

Close to the square is the amazing St Basil's Cathedral. With its colourful onion-shaped domes, it looks just like a fairytale palace.

Firebird
This magical creature from Russian fairy tales has fiery red and orange feathers.

Toy space rocket
The Russian cosmonaut Yuri Gagarin was the first person to journey into outer space.

Gingerbread man
Freshly baked ginger biscuits served with hot tea is a popular Russian delicacy.

Brown bear
Brown bears live in Russia's forests. This one has snuck into town to join in the fun!

Ganesh Festival

MUMBAI, INDIA

It's the final day of this Hindu festival celebrating the birth of the beloved elephant-headed god Ganesh. There is loud music and dancing, and the sweet smell of festival food fills the air!

Things to Spot

Ganesh idol
Lord Ganesh is the god of wisdom, happiness and good fortune.

Modaka
These sweet coconut dumplings are said to be Lord Ganesh's favourite treat.

Red flower garland
Gifts of food and flowers are added to the statues to help bring good luck.

Goddess Parvati
So the legend goes, Ganesh was created out of earth by his mother, Parvati.

Thousands of clay statues of Ganesh – big and small – are carried through the streets in a big procession, then dipped into the ocean.

Monkey
Monkeys are sacred animals to Hindus. They roam the streets of many Indian cities.

Sadhu
A sadhu is a holy man who spends his days praying and meditating.

Sitar
The sitar is one of the most well-known Indian musical instruments.

Shehnai flute
Musicians play drums, cymbals and other traditional instruments, like this flute.

In China, every year is represented by one of twelve animals: rat, ox, tiger, rabbit, dragon, snake, horse, goat, monkey, rooster, dog or pig.

人咸自在院聖生封防之權

樞要零育狸寗化陰陽之經

福

福

Chinese New Year

BEIJING, CHINA

New Year is China's biggest festival – a time when people come together to welcome the coming of spring and to wish each other good luck, wealth and happiness. Homes and temples are decorated with red lanterns, and there is feasting, music, fireworks and spectacular dragon and lion dances.

Things to Spot

Incense sticks
These fragrant sticks are lit to help bring good luck for the new year ahead.

Red envelope
Lucky red envelopes are filled with money and given to children as gifts.

Lucky fish
Fish are a symbol of good fortune. A pair of fish is said to bring 'double good luck'.

Door god
Pictures of fearsome door gods are hung on doorways to scare away demons.

Conical hat
These pointed hats were once worn by officials from the Qing dynasty.

Pot-balancer
Chinese acrobats perform amazing tricks, such as balancing pots on their heads!

Yo-yo
The Chinese yo-yo is one of the oldest toys. It was invented more than 2000 years ago.

Steamed buns
Food stalls sell festival snacks, such as these delicious steamed buns.

Rush Hour

TOKYO, JAPAN

It's rush hour in downtown Tokyo. Neon signs
light up the sky, and the streets are filled with
shoppers. This flashy city is renowned for its
high-tech inventions and super-speedy bullet
trains – some of the fastest trains in the world!

Climb down the subway steps to catch a train or shop in the underground shopping mall.

Things to Spot

Lucky cat souvenir
This waving cat is thought to bring happiness and good fortune to its owner.

Karaoke
A visit to Tokyo isn't complete until you've sung your heart out at karaoke!

Sumo wrestlers
Sumo wrestlers have to eat a LOT of rice and noodles to get this big.

Singing toilet
This amazing high-tech toilet plays music when you flush it!

Selfie stick
See if you can find the happy shopper trying out his new selfie stick!

Noodle restaurant
Noodles are a popular Japanese dish. You eat them with wooden chopsticks.

Pink facemask
In Japan it's considered polite to cover your nose and mouth if you have a cold.

Train pusher
This pushy station worker is helping to squeeze people onto the busy trains.

Running Festival

SYDNEY, AUSTRALIA

The sun is out, and Sydney's Running Festival is in full swing. Runners of all ages can take part and see the sights of the city's harbour along the way.

Things to Spot

Whale
Enormous humpback whales sometimes shelter in the bays around the harbour.

Crocodile
This little croc must be lost. They usually live in Northern Australia and can grow to 6 m (20 ft)!

Surfer
Sydneysiders love to surf. There are loads of lovely beaches nearby to practise on.

Didgeridoo
This long wooden wind instrument was invented by the Aboriginal peoples of Australia.

Can you see the Harbour Bridge and Opera House? They are two of the city's most famous attractions.

YOU CAN DO IT!

KEEP U

Boomerang
Aboriginal people used these throwing sticks for hunting emus and kangaroos.

Uluru poster
This massive red rock in the centre of Australia was formed over 500 million ago.

Waterskier
There are lots of fun things to do in the harbour. You can dolphin watch, sail a boat or waterski!

Running medal
This competitor must have run this race before. He already has a medal!

More things to spot

Here are some bonus objects for you to find in each city, but before you do, see if you can guess where each item comes from. The answers can be found at the bottom of the page.

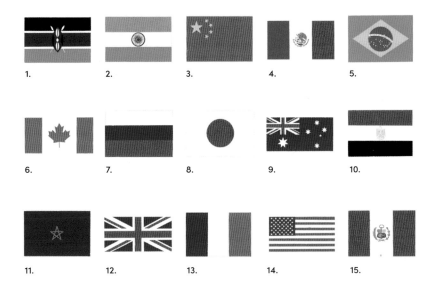

FLAGS

Every country has its own flag with special colours and patterns. You might see flags waving at festivals or sporting events, or fluttering from buildings. Can you match the flag to the country?

A. Canada
B. USA
C. Mexico
D. Brazil
E. Peru
F. Morocco
G. Egypt
H. Kenya

I. United Kingdom
J. France
K. Russia
L. India
M. China
N. Japan
O. Australia

LANDMARKS

1. St Basil's Cathedral

2. National Park

3. Opera House

4. Mount Fuji

5. Koutoubia Mosque

6. Machu Picchu

7. Christ Redeemer statue

8. Gateway of India

9. Statue of Liberty

10. Eiffel Tower

11. Metropolitan Cathedral

12. Nelson's Column

13. CN Tower

14. Dongyue Temple

15. Pyramids of Giza

Cities are full of buildings and statues, old and new. Some have mountains or other natural features that people come from miles around to see. Do you know where you'd find these famous landmarks?

A. Toronto
B. New York
C. Mexico City
D. Rio de Janeiro
E. Near Cusco
F. Marrakesh
G. Cairo
H. Nairobi

I. London
J. Paris
K. Moscow
L. Mumbai
M. Beijing
N. Tokyo
O. Sydney

CLOTHES

In some cities, people wear cosy clothes to keep them warm. In other places, they stay cool in the hot sun by wearing clothes that are light and airy. Some outfits are traditional and have been worn by locals for hundreds of years. Can you guess where these are from?

A. Toronto
B. New York
C. Mexico City
D. Rio de Janeiro
E. Cusco
F. Marrakesh
G. Cairo
H. Nairobi

I. London
J. Paris
K. Moscow
L. Mumbai
M. Beijing
N. Tokyo
O. Sydney

1. Pearly Queen outfit

2. Maasai shuka

3. Beret

4. Baseball jacket

5. Hijab (head scarf)

6. Hanfu dress

7. Carnival costume

8. Sombrero

9. Kimono

10. Cork hat

11. Sari

12. Ushanka ear-flap hat

13. Warm coat and woolly hat

14. Poncho

15. Djellaba and fez

ANIMALS

Cities can be home to all kinds of animals – from rascally raccoons that rummage through bins to colourful birds that zoom above the rooftops. Can you match the animal to the city?

A. Toronto
B. New York
C. Mexico City
D. Rio de Janeiro
E. Cusco
F. Marrakesh
G. Cairo
H. Nairobi

I. London
J. Paris
K. Moscow
L. Mumbai
M. Beijing
N. Tokyo
O. Sydney

1. Raccoon dog

2. Cockatoo

3. Cow

4. Mandarin duck

5. Red squirrel

6. Poodle

7. Parrot

8. Stork

9. Camel

10. Bald eagle

11. Llama

12. Pigeon

13. Hummingbird

14. Giraffe

15. Raccoon

FOOD

It's always nice to sample the local dishes when you visit a new city. See if you can guess where you would eat these different foods.

 1. Fish and chips

 2. Taco

 3. Tagine

 4. Caviar and pancakes

 5. Simit bread

 6. Croissant

 7. Coconut

 8. Sushi

 9. Maple syrup

 10. Hot dog

 11. Barbecued prawns

 12. Corn

 13. Pancake rolls

 14. Samosa

 15. Bananas

A. Toronto
B. New York
C. Mexico City
D. Rio de Janeiro
E. Cusco
F. Marrakesh
G. Cairo
H. Nairobi
I. London
J. Paris
K. Moscow
L. Mumbai
M. Beijing
N. Tokyo
O. Sydney

SOUVENIRS

No trip is complete until you've bought a souvenir to remind you of your visit or to give to your friends. Where might you pick up some of these local treasures?

 1. Tutankhamun statue

 2. Nesting dolls

 3. Teapot

 4. Robot dog

 5. Panpipes

 6. Kangaroo toy

 7. Lucha libre mask

 8. Mini totem pole

 9. Maasai shield and spear

 10. Spices

 11. Perfume

 12. Maracas

 13. City snowglobe

 14. Lantern

 15. Bollywood poster

A. Toronto
B. New York
C. Mexico City
D. Rio de Janeiro
E. Cusco
F. Marrakesh
G. Cairo
H. Nairobi
I. London
J. Paris
K. Moscow
L. Mumbai
M. Beijing
N. Tokyo
O. Sydney

Answers

Did you spot all of the hidden objects on each page?
Top marks if you found Cat and Bird in every city, too!

ICE RINK
Toronto, Canada

1. Orange earmuffs
2. Beaver
3. Moose
4. Ice hockey stick
5. Dreamcatcher
6. Maple taffy
7. Snowshoes
8. Inuksuk

EXTRA SPOTS

9. Canadian flag
10. CN Tower
11. Warm coat and woolly hat
12. Raccoon
13. Maple syrup
14. Mini totem pole

NEW YEAR'S EVE
New York City, USA

1. Clock and ball
2. Big Apple
3. Policeman
4. Cheerleader
5. Pretzel
6. American footballer
7. Souvenir T-shirt
8. Foam hand

EXTRA SPOTS

9. US flag
10. Statue of Liberty
11. Baseball jacket
12. Bald eagle
13. Hot dog
14. City snow globe

DAY OF THE DEAD
Mexico City, Mexico

1. Smart skeleton
2. Altar
3. Bread of the dead
4. Pair of shoes
5. Water jug
6. Pozole stew
7. Mariachi band
8. Aztec emperor

EXTRA SPOTS

9. Mexican flag
10. Metropolitan Cathedral
11. Sombrero
12. Hummingbird
13. Taco
14. Lucha libre mask

INTI RAYMI
Cusco, Peru

1. Sun god
2. Inca emperor
3. Inca priest
4. Mandolin
5. Sweepers
6. Bowl of chicha
7. Puma statue
8. Condor

EXTRA SPOTS

9. Peruvian flag
10. Machu Picchu
11. Poncho
12. Llama
13. Corn
14. Panpipes

CARNIVAL
Rio de Janeiro, Brazil

1. Carnival float
2. Pink drum
3. Samba whistle
4. Red shaker stick
5. Monkey
6. Football player
7. Yellow headdress
8. Lost flip-flop (and its owner)

EXTRA SPOTS

9. Brazilian flag
10. Christ Redeemer statue
11. Carnival costume
12. Parrot
13. Coconut
14. Maracas

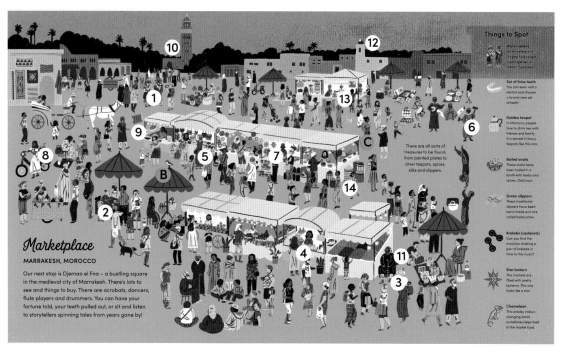

MARKETPLACE
Marrakesh, Morocco

1. Water sellers
2. Set of false teeth
3. Golden teapot
4. Boiled snails
5. Green slippers
6. Krakebs (castanets)
7. Star lantern
8. Chameleon

EXTRA SPOTS

9. Moroccan flag
10. Koutoubia Mosque
11. Djellaba and fez
12. Stork
13. Tagine
14. Spices

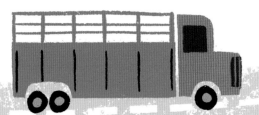

The Pyramids of Giza
CAIRO, EGYPT

Rising out of the golden desert, the pyramids of Giza were built thousands of years ago for ancient Egyptian kings and queens. People come from all over the world to peep inside these magnificent tombs.

The tombs were once filled with objects for the pharaohs to use in the afterlife but over the years they have been raided by thieves. Today, you can buy gifts that look like the ancient treasures.

Things to Spot

Papyrus scroll
Papyrus is a kind of paper made from reeds used in ancient Egypt for writing.

Sand bottle
Bottles filled with desert sand are a popular souvenir. This one has pyramids inside.

Statue of Anubis
Anubis was the Egyptian god of the dead. He guarded the gates of the underworld.

Falcon
The falcon was a sacred bird to the Egyptians and thought to have protective powers.

Statue of Isis
Isis was a caring goddess who protected the sick and helped crops to grow.

Egyptian ibis
This long-necked bird is said to be the reincarnation of Thoth – the god of knowledge.

Egyptian mummy
An Egyptian mummy wrapped up in bandages is being a tourist for the day. Can you find it?

Archaeologist
Archaeologists are scientists who study objects from the past.

THE PYRAMIDS OF GIZA
Cairo, Egypt

1. Papyrus scroll
2. Sand bottle
3. Statue of Anubis
4. Falcon
5. Statue of Isis
6. Egyptian ibis
7. Egyptian mummy
8. Archaeologist

EXTRA SPOTS

9. Egyptian flag
10. Pyramids of Giza
11. Hijab (head scarf)
12. Camel
13. Simit bread
14. Tutankhamun statue

Maasai Market
NAIROBI, KENYA

Are you ready to haggle? This colourful market is crammed with hand-crafted souvenirs made by the local people. There are wooden carvings of wild beasts, paintings, drums and tribal masks. What will you buy first?

The Nairobi National Park on the edge of the city is home to all kinds of animals, including giraffes, lions and leopards.

Things to Spot

Lion sculpture
This wooden carving is shaped like a lion – the largest of Africa's big cats.

Zebra mask
Zebras look a bit like stripey horses. They are hunted by lions and crocodiles.

Maize cob
Look out for street vendors selling fresh fruit and grilled corn cobs.

Kikoi
This lady is using a traditional cloth called a kikoi to carry her baby on her back.

Jewellery maker
Can you see the lady threading beads to make jewellery?

Baobab tree
This strange-looking tree with a bulging trunk grows on the African grasslands.

Maasai warrior
The Maasai people live on the African plains in houses made from mud and sticks.

Tribal mask
Wooden masks were used by African tribes to scare away their enemies.

MAASAI MARKET
Nairobi, Kenya

1. Lion sculpture
2. Zebra mask
3. Maize cob
4. Kikoi
5. Jewellery maker
6. Baobab tree
7. Maasai warrior
8. Tribal mask

EXTRA SPOTS

9. Kenyan flag
10. Nairobi National Park
11. Maasai shuka
12. Giraffe
13. Bananas
14. Maasai shield and spear

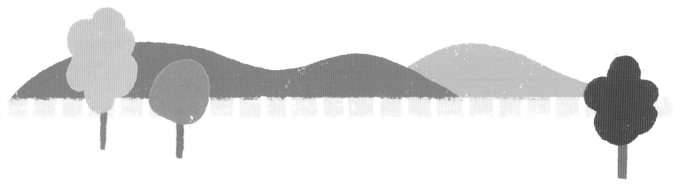

TRAFALGAR SQUARE
London, UK

1. Telephone box
2. Crown jewels
3. Corgi
4. Street performer
5. Palace guard
6. Big Ben
7. Two lion statues
8. Red fox

EXTRA SPOTS

9. UK flag
10. Nelson's Column
11. Pearly Queen outfit
12. Pigeon
13. Fish and chips
14. Teapot

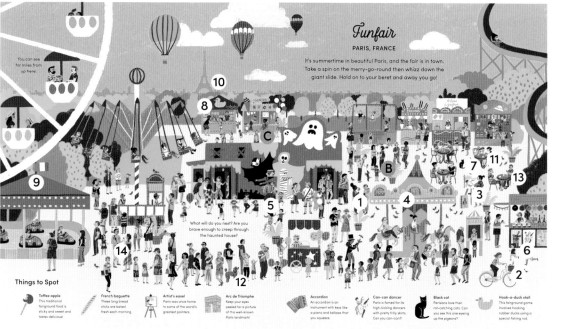

FUNFAIR
Paris, France

1. Toffee apple
2. French baguette
3. Artist's easel
4. Arc de Triomphe
5. Accordion
6. Can-can dancer
7. Black cat
8. Hook-a-duck stall

EXTRA SPOTS

9. French flag
10. Eiffel Tower
11. Beret
12. Poodle
13. Croissant
14. Perfume

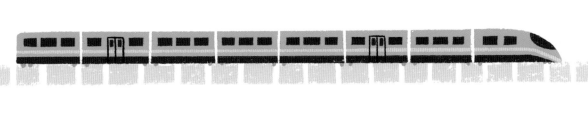

CHRISTMAS MARKET
Moscow, Russia

1. Snow Maiden
2. Samovar
3. Space dog toy
4. Hand muff
5. Firebird
6. Toy space rocket
7. Gingerbread man
8. Brown bear

EXTRA SPOTS

9. Russian flag
10. St Basil's Cathedral
11. Ushanka ear-flap hat
12. Red squirrel
13. Caviar and pancakes
14. Nesting dolls

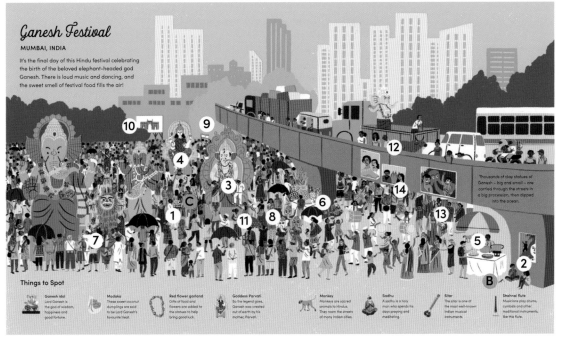

GANESH FESTIVAL
Mumbai, India

1. Ganesh idol
2. Modaka
3. Red flower garland
4. Goddess Parvati
5. Monkey
6. Sadhu
7. Sitar
8. Shehnai flute

EXTRA SPOTS

9. Indian flag
10. Gateway of India
11. Sari
12. Cow
13. Samosa
14. Bollywood poster

CHINESE NEW YEAR
Beijing, China

1. Incense sticks
2. Red envelope
3. Lucky fish
4. Door god
5. Conical hat
6. Pot-balancer
7. Yo-yo
8. Steamed buns

EXTRA SPOTS

9. Chinese flag
10. Dongyue Temple
11. Hanfu dress
12. Mandarin duck
13. Pancake rolls
14. Lantern

In China, every year is represented by one of twelve animals: rat, ox, tiger, rabbit, dragon, snake, horse, goat, monkey, rooster, dog or pig.

Things to Spot

Incense sticks
These fragrant sticks are lit to help bring good luck for the new year ahead.

Red envelope
Lucky red envelopes are filled with money and given to children as gifts.

Lucky fish
Fish are a symbol of good fortune. A pair of fish is said to bring 'double luck'.

Door god
Pictures of fearsome door gods are hung on doorways to scare away demons.

Conical hat
These pointed hats were worn by officials from the Qing dynasty.

Pot-balancer
Chinese acrobats perform amazing tricks, such as balancing pots on their heads!

Yo-yo
The Chinese yo-yo is one of the oldest toys. It was invented more than 2000 years ago.

Steamed buns
Food stalls sell festival snacks, such as these delicious steamed buns.

Chinese New Year

BEIJING, CHINA

New Year is China's biggest festival – a time when people come together to welcome the coming of spring and to wish each other good luck, wealth and happiness. Homes and temples are decorated with red lanterns, and there is feasting, music, fireworks and spectacular dragon and lion dances.

RUSH HOUR
Tokyo, Japan

1. Lucky cat souvenir
2. Karaoke
3. Sumo wrestlers
4. Singing toilet
5. Selfie stick
6. Noodle restaurant
7. Pink face mask
8. Train pusher

EXTRA SPOTS

9. Japanese flag
10. Mount Fuji
11. Kimono
12. Raccoon dog
13. Sushi
14. Robot dog

Rush Hour

TOKYO, JAPAN

It's rush hour in downtown Tokyo. Neon signs light up the sky, and the streets are filled with shoppers. This flashy city is renowned for its high-tech inventions and super-speedy bullet trains – some of the fastest trains in the world!

Things to Spot

Lucky cat souvenir
This waving cat is thought to bring happiness and good fortune to its owner.

Karaoke
A visit to Tokyo isn't complete until you've sung your heart out at karaoke!

Sumo wrestlers
Sumo wrestlers have to eat a LOT of rice and noodles to get this big.

Singing toilet
This amazing high-tech toilet plays music when you flush it!

Selfie stick
See if you can find the happy shopper trying out his new selfie stick!

Noodle restaurant
Noodles are a popular Japanese dish. You eat them with wooden chopsticks.

Pink face mask
In Japan it's considered polite to cover your nose and mouth if you have a cold.

Train pusher
This pushy station worker is helping to squeeze people onto the busy trains.

Climb down the subway steps to catch a train or shop in the underground shopping mall.

Running Festival

SYDNEY, AUSTRALIA

The sun is out, and Sydney's Running Festival is in full swing. Runners of all ages can take part and see the sights of the city's harbour along the way.

Can you see the Harbour Bridge and Opera House? They are two of the city's most famous attractions.

Things to Spot

Whale
Enormous humpback whales sometimes shelter in the bays around the harbour.

Crocodile
This little croc must be lost. They usually live in Northern Australia and can grow to 6 m (20 ft)!

Surfer
Sydneysiders love to surf. There are loads of lovely beaches nearby to practise on.

Didgeridoo
This long wooden wind instrument was invented by the Aboriginal peoples of Australia.

Boomerang
Aboriginal people used these throwing sticks for hunting emus and kangaroos.

Uluru poster
This massive red rock in the centre of Australia was formed over 500 million ago.

Waterskier
There are lots of fun things to do in the harbour. You can dolphin watch, sail a boat or waterski!

Running medal
This competitor must have run this race before. He already has a medal!

RUNNING FESTIVAL
Sydney, Australia

1. Whale
2. Crocodile
3. Surfer
4. Didgeridoo
5. Boomerang
6. Uluru poster
7. Waterskier
8. Running medal

EXTRA SPOTS

9. Australian flag
10. Opera House
11. Cork hat
12. Cockatoo
13. Barbecued shrimp
14. Kangaroo toy

About the authors

KATE BAKER
Author & Editor

Kate is a children's book editor and author who divides her time between London in the UK, and sunny Spain. She loves exploring old castles and ancient ruins, and collecting weird and wonderful facts about the world.

SANDRA DE LA PRADA
Illustrator

Sandra is an illustrator who lives in Barcelona, Spain, with her family and her two cats, Chicho and Rudo. What she likes most is escaping to nature, going to the movies and painting with her son.

Published in October 2019 by Lonely Planet Global Ltd

CRN: 554153
ISBN: 978 1 78868 617 4

www.lonelyplanetkids.com
© Lonely Planet 2019

10 9 8 7 6 5 4 3 2 1

Printed in China

Publishing Director: Piers Pickard
Publisher: Hanna Otero
Art Director: Andy Mansfield
Commissioning Editor: Joe Fullman
Designer: Tina García
Author and Editor: Kate Baker
Print Production: Lisa Ford

Lonely Planet Offices

AUSTRALIA
The Malt Store, Level 3, 551 Swanston St, Carlton, Victoria 3053
T: 03 8379 8000

IRELAND
Digital Depot, Roe Lane (off Thomas St), Digital Hub,
Dublin 8, D08 TCV4

USA
124 Linden St, Oakland, CA 94607
T: 510 250 6400

UK
240 Blackfriars Rd, London, SE1 8NW
T: 020 3771 5100

STAY IN TOUCH
lonelyplanet.com/contact